Table of Con

CW00497499

INTJ: Understanding & Relating with the Mastermind

MBTI Personality Types Series

By: Clayton Geoffreys

Foreword

Have you ever been curious about why you behave certain ways? Well I know I have always pondered this question. When I first learned about psychology in high school, I immediately was hooked. Learning about the inner workings of the human mind fascinated me. Human beings are some of the most impressive species to ever walk on this earth. Over the years, one thing I've learned from my life experiences is that having a high degree of self-awareness is critical to get to where you want to go in life and to achieve what you want to accomplish. A person who is not self-aware is a person who lives life blindly, accepting what some label as fate. I began intensely studying psychology to better understand myself, and through my journey, I discovered the Myers Brigg Type Indicator (MBTI), a popular personality test that distinguishes between sixteen types of individuals. I hope to cover some of the most prevalent personality types of the MBTI test and share my findings with you through a series of books. Rather than just reading this for the sake of reading it though, I want you to reflect on the information that will be shared with you. Hopefully from reading *INTJ: Understanding & Relating with the Mastermind*, I can pass along some of the abundance of information I have learned about INTJs in general, how they view the world, as well as their greatest strengths and weaknesses. Thank you for purchasing my book. Hope you enjoy and if you do, please do not forget to leave a review! Also, check out my website at claytongeoffreys.com to join my exclusive list where I let you know about my latest books. To thank you for your purchase, you can go to my site to download a free copy of *33 Life Lessons: Success Principles, Career Advice & Habits of Successful People*. In the book, you'll learn from some of the greatest thought leaders of different industries on what it takes to become successful and how to live a great life.

Cheers,

Clayton Geffrey

An Introduction to MBTI

Everyone wants to be happy. In fact, many people spend hundreds of dollars on self-help books, inspirational seminars, and how-to guides in an attempt to achieve long-lasting happiness. That said, happiness may mean different things for different people. One person might find it in career advancement and financial stability, while another might find it in building a family. Because of this, it's almost impossible to find a one-size-fits-all guide that would work for everyone. This is one of the reasons why the Myers-Briggs Type Indicator (MBTI) is so important.

Are you reserved or outgoing? Are you pragmatic or future-focused? Do you lead with your head or follow your feelings? Do you like guidelines and structure or are you more laid-back and easygoing? These are a few of the things that the MBTI can help you determine. The Myers-Briggs Type Indicator test is a questionnaire designed to assess a person's personality type. It targets the four dimensions of an individual's personality (extroversion and introversion, thinking and feeling, intuition and sensing, perceiving and judging) and combines each dimension's results to identify their personality type. There are sixteen personality types that can be classified into four temperaments: Guardians (ISFJ, ESFJ, ISTJ, ESTJ), Rationals (ENTJ, INTJ, INTP, ENTP), Artisans (ESTP, ISTP, ISFP, ESFP), and Idealists (ENFP, INFP, INFJ, ENFJ). The different temperaments are a combination of the types that possess the most similarities.

The sixteen personality types differ from each other in so many ways. Some types are more emotional than others. There are types that are more outgoing than the rest. Each type sees the world and makes decisions differently. Each has its own unique set of innate strengths and weaknesses. The MBTI operates based on the idea that every single thing you do is a result of your personality framework. Do you have high expectations of people? Do you find it hard to say no when a friend asks you for a favor? Do you prefer spending time alone? These are only a few things that can be explained by understanding your personality type.

The MBTI assessment was first published in 1962. It was developed by Isabel Briggs-Myers and her mother, Katharine Cook Briggs. The mother-daughter duo began their work on the MBTI after extensively studying the theories of Carl Jung. According to Jung, there are four primary functions that we use in making decisions and perceiving the world around us. These functions determine our personality framework. Briggs and Myers took those theories one step further and created a set of questions that would ascertain an individual's personality type. Their original goal was to help women find jobs during the war. Since then, the MBTI has grown to become the most popular personality assessment in the world.

For these reasons, the MBTI is an important and essential tool for success. By knowing your MBTI personality type, you no longer have to rely on vague and generalized guides to achieve happiness. After all, true and lasting happiness stems from a true understanding of one's self.

The Four Dimensions of the MBTI

Consider this. When making choices in your day-to-day life, how do you arrive at a decision? Are you the kind of person who makes a list of the pros and cons before making a choice? Or do you just go with what your gut tells you? This is just one of the dimensions of the MBTI.

According to the MBTI, an individual's personality can be divided into four dimensions. Each dimension is responsible for a particular cognitive function: how social interaction affects your energy levels (introversion vs. extroversion), how you gather data from your surroundings (intuition vs. sensing), how you decide things (thinking vs. feeling), and how you move about in the world (judging vs. perceiving).

Although it can be argued that both qualities in a certain dimension can exist in one individual, one attribute will always be more dominant. For instance,

8

you may identify as both a thinker and a feeler, but emotions tend to play a bigger role in how you make decisions. In this case, feeling is your dominant function.

1. Introversion (I) vs. Extroversion (E)

Among the four dimensions, this is the most well-known. However, most people assume that introverts are quiet and shy, while extroverts love being the center of attention. Although these things can be true, there's so much more to it than just that. This dimension actually refers to how social interaction affects your energy levels.

If your dominant function is introversion, solitude and isolation energize you. It's not that you do not like being around other people, it's just that being in a crowd for too long is exhausting for you. You need to spend time by yourself to get your energy levels back up again.

If extroversion is your dominant function, you are energized by being surrounded by other people. You love meeting new people and engaging in conversations. Being alone for too long brings your energy levels down.

2. Intuition (N) vs. Sensing (S)

The second dimension is all about how you gather information from your surroundings. It's either through sensing or through intuition.

If your dominant function is sensing, that means you are pragmatic and logical. As the term 'sensing' indicates, you rely on your five physical senses to assess what's happening around you. You do not like jumping to conclusions if there's no physical evidence to back it up.

On the other hand, if your dominant function is intuition, you are perfectly comfortable with going with your gut. You have the ability to read between the lines and see connections between certain things that are not immediately apparent. You're more of a visionary than a pragmatist.

3. Thinking (T) vs. Feeling (F)

The third dimension refers to the process by which you make decisions. What do you do with all the data your second dimension has just gathered?

If your dominant function is thinking, you use your head. It's likely that you list down the pros and cons of each choice before making a decision. You are able to temporarily detach yourself from a situation so that you can arrive at a choice that is objectively sound.

On the other hand, if your dominant function is feeling, you're the type of person who uses emotions. You follow your heart, and can be very compassionate and empathetic toward the feelings of others. In fact, you would much rather be thought of as illogical than be called unsympathetic and unkind.

11

4. Judging (J) vs. Perceiving (P)

The last dimension refers to how you move about in the world. A common misconception is that an inclination toward judging makes you a judgmental person. However, judging means something very different when it comes to MBTI.

If judging is your dominant function, it means you are organized and live a life of structure. You dislike chaos and disorderliness. This not only manifests in how neat you keep your surroundings, but also in the way you respect and adhere to guidelines and rules. You love planning, and it's likely that you follow a daily schedule.

On the other hand, if your dominant function is perceiving, you're more laid-back and carefree. Rules and routine bore you. You do not like feeling tied down by people or responsibilities. In fact, you like keeping your options open, and you're able to switch plans at a minute's notice. This gives you the ability to adapt to changing circumstances. It also makes you more open-minded.

Why is the Myers-Briggs Type Indicator Significant?

The Myers-Briggs Type Indicator test has undeniably grown in significance since its inception. In fact, most people who take the test have reported that they now possess a greater sense of self-awareness and understanding. While it's true that there are other personality assessments that you can take, no test is as in-depth and reliable as the MBTI.

The great thing about the MBTI is that it not only helps you identify your personality type, but it also gives you detailed information about the inner workings of your mind. Upon receiving your MBTI test results, you will gain insight into why you behave a certain way during particular situations and why you perceive things the way you do. It will also help you identify your natural strengths and weaknesses, as well as how to nourish and overcome them. This knowledge

14

can be extremely empowering, because it allows you to make more informed decisions about your career, work habits, and personal relationships.

Not only can you take a peek into your own mind, you can also get a glimpse of what makes other people tick. As a result, you can build more harmonious relationships with the people you interact with. Identifying and understanding someone else's personality type can be a big Eureka moment. It can give you insight into their interests, motivations, and overall behavior. It can also enable you to create more open lines of communication, because like everything else, a person's preferred communication style is inextricably tied to their personality type. This is extremely useful when it comes to friendships, romance, and family, but it's just as helpful in any social situation.

The MBTI test has also been used in a number of fields, such as in the workplace or in school. Knowing your personality type can help you make better choices regarding your career. It can also help you adjust your work or study habits depending on what works best for you. Furthermore, it can give you a better understanding of your colleagues or peers. Even large organizations and corporations have begun using the MBTI test as part of their screening process. According to them, the MBTI has proven to be essential in determining whether a candidate's personality type is aligned with their mission and objectives.

For all these reasons, the Myers-Briggs Type Indicator test is extremely significant.

Uncovering the "Masterminds": Who is an INTJ?

INTJ is one of the 16 different personality types according to the MBTI test. The acronym stands for Introversion, Intuition, Thinking, and Judging. One of the rarest personality types, INTJs make up only 1.5% of the general population.

The cognitive functions of an INTJ are as follows:

- Dominant: Introverted Intuition (Ni) - The dominant function refers to the role you are most comfortable with. If you are an INTJ, your dominant function is Introverted Intuition (Ni). In general, people who are intuitive process information through impressions and possibilities. Introverted Intuition gives you an inner sense of what will happen next. You have the ability to see connections between things, allowing you to see patterns and sequences that others might overlook.

17

- Auxiliary: Extroverted Thinking (Te) - The auxiliary function exists to serve and expand the dominant function. If you are an INTJ, your auxiliary function is Extroverted Thinking (Te). Thinkers use logic and objective analysis to analyze and categorize their thoughts. When combined with your dominant (Ni) function, Extroverted Thinking enables you to form logical conclusions about the patterns and sequences around you. It involves the organization of thoughts and ideas before they are spoken out loud.

- Tertiary: Introverted Feeling (Fi) - The tertiary function is less developed than the auxiliary and dominant functions, however, it may become more pronounced over time. If you are an INTJ, your tertiary function is Introverted Feeling (Fi). Because your feelings are focused inward, you may not express them as often or as easily, but you inherently possess a radar that allows you to see inside other people and understand what they are feeling.

- Inferior: Extroverted Intuition (Se) - The inferior function is often referred to as the Achilles' heel. It's the role you are least comfortable with. If you are an INTJ, your inferior function is Extroverted Sensing (Se). This function deals with living in the present, relying only on what you can process with your five senses. As a future-focused INTJ, it's unlikely that you will feel comfortable with this process.

If you are an INTJ, you are an analytical, strategic, and responsible individual who possesses strong leadership skills. As an introvert, you value your privacy and solitude. As an intuitive, you are able to form connections between seemingly unrelated things. Due to your inclination toward thinking, you are decisive and logical. Finally, the judging side of your personality allows you to operate against a backdrop of structure and organization.

INTJs are part of the Rational temperament group. All rationals are excellent planners, but none are as efficient as INTJs. In fact, INTJs are often called Masterminds, Architects, or Strategists. Because of your ability to see patterns and sequences, you know exactly how one action will lead to another, and another, and so on. Furthermore, your organizational skills enable you to break down plans into clear steps. You're the type of person who always has a back-up plan. Even though your Plan A is always solid, you make sure that Plans B, C, and D are just as efficient.

Even though you have strong leadership skills, you are not hungry for the spotlight. In fact, you are perfectly content to stay in the background. That is, until the current leader proves to be inefficient. When that happens, you eagerly take a step forward to make sure that the plan is successfully followed. For you, efficiency is of utmost importance. When you see that a certain aspect of a project does not work well, you immediately take charge to ensure that no resources are wasted. Although you welcome theoretical discussions and are open to new possibilities, you still choose to make decisions based on extensive research and analysis.

Because INTJs are so rare, it can be quite a challenge for you to seek out like-minded people. Others might even see you as a walking paradox. This is true. You can be extremely idealistic and simultaneously cynical. Your mysteriousness and strong personality often draw people to you. However, you can be quite picky when it comes to the people you surround yourself with. Small talk and social graces do not interest you at all. In fact, you see most social conventions as needless and silly. Overall, you see life like a giant game of chess. You are constantly coming up with new tactics and strategies to succeed in any situation. For these reasons, you are often misunderstood. In fact, people with more sensitive personalities might see you as cold and calculating. In popular culture, most fictional villains are modeled after INTJs.

Why are INTJs Indispensable Leaders?

INTJs are natural-born leaders and are extremely comfortable taking on authoritative positions. As an INTJ leader, your quiet and reserved demeanor makes you come across as approachable and welcoming (introversion). You have the ability to plan ahead and see the big picture (intuition). You are very decisive and make decisions based on research and analysis (thinking). You are also highly organized and responsible (judging).

In general, you are perfectly happy to let someone else take the lead, as long as tasks and projects are carried out effectively. In fact, you have great respect for leaders who are efficient and capable. You do not feel the need to take control, unless you see holes in efficiency. When that happens, you will not hesitate to take charge, so that everything continues to run smoothly.

23

When you step into a leadership position, you value efficiency above all else. You do not want your team's efforts and resources to go to waste. You are also very objective, and you have a clear vision of what needs to get done and how to do it. Unlike other judging personalities, you are very adaptable. You are comfortable with changing plans if the circumstances call for it. This is also the reason you make sure that there are solid back-up plans in case Plan A does not work out.

You are an excellent strategist and mastermind, and this shines through in your management style. You are constantly coming up with new ideas and approaches to make the organization run more efficiently. When you encounter new suggestions, you objectively measure them against the current course of action to decide which will be more effective. You see the big picture as you would a jigsaw puzzle, and you enjoy the process of assessing which pieces will fit.

Most personalities with the judging trait rely heavily on rules and pre-existing guidelines. INTJs are different. You will readily bypass established protocols, as long as the new idea is backed up by research and a rational explanation. The same goes for your own thoughts and decisions. You believe that there is always room for improvement, and you are not averse to welcoming input from your colleagues and team members.

As a leader, you prefer treating your subordinates as equals, and you respect their individual skills and abilities. As such, you are great at spotting who will do well at which task and can delegate appropriately. That said, you expect your team to be independent thinkers who do not require constant supervision. You tend to have high standards that other people with different personality types might find difficult to live up to.

You're not the type whose bias can be bought through emotional ties. Personal relationships are not necessary or important to you when it comes to your career. You have no patience for people who are inefficient and lazy. You are not impressed by people who try to win you over by wanting to be your friend. In the workplace, the only way to impress you is by delivering efficient results.

The 7 Greatest Strengths of an INTJ

As an INTJ, you are a treasure chest of many remarkable qualities. You are intelligent, responsible, and highly strategic. You possess the ability to see a situation from every possible angle, and you're able to formulate a plan depending on the circumstances.

Nurture your natural strengths and abilities and be the best version of yourself you can possibly be. Here are some of the natural skills and strengths of an INTJ.

1. Determination

Not much fazes you. You are driven, dedicated, and strong-willed. No task is too difficult and no project is too daunting once you set your mind to it. Because of this, you tend to do well in any pursuit you devote yourself to. This persistence helps you keep your eye on the goal, even in the face of challenges. You do not mind spending hours and exerting a lot of effort just to complete the task at hand.

2. Strategic and Imaginative Mind

As an INTJ, you possess a gifted mind when it comes to strategizing and decision-making. As mentioned earlier, you have the ability to view a situation from every possible perspective. The flexibility of your thinking enables you to plan for every possible outcome. What's even more interesting is that you genuinely enjoy this process. You love finishing puzzles and solving problems, and you embrace intellectual challenges.

3. Self-Confidence

INTJs possess a high level of self-confidence. Not many people can say that. Your confidence stems from your rational way of thinking. Once you reach a conclusion, you see no reason to doubt or question your beliefs. As a result, you prefer open and direct conversations that are not littered with social expectations and niceties. Your confidence is also a product of your intelligence. You enjoy learning about the things that interest you, and once you become an expert on a certain subject, nothing can take away your confidence regarding the matter.

4. Open-Mindedness

As an INTJ, you are very receptive to new ideas and views. You are not afraid of the unfamiliar. Although you are extremely confident about your own beliefs, you readily embrace suggestions and input that can make things in your life more efficient. You do not mind being proven wrong once in a while. You know that there's always room for improvement, and there's always a way to make things run more smoothly. That said, you never lose your rational thinking. The new ideas you embrace have to be supported by logical explanations and thorough research.

5. Jack of All Trades

Because of your determination and intelligence, you have the ability to learn a multitude of skills and abilities. As long as you set your mind to it, there's nothing you're not able to do. As a result, it's common for INTJs to be jacks and jills of all trades. When encountering something new, you're able to use your strategic thinking to understand how it works and how you can do it as well. In fact, INTJs can excel in any career, hobby, or interest they choose.

6. Intelligence

When we talk about intelligence, it goes further than just an individual's I.Q. For instance, an INTJ with an average I.Q. will be able to understand theories and concepts that are far beyond what their I.Q. appears to be. As an INTJ, your flexible and strategic mind is constantly working and learning. You are always analyzing how things work, how they can be made to perform more efficiently, and how to apply this knowledge to other aspects of your life.

7. Love for Learning

INTJs love learning new things. If you are an INTJ, you are likely a voracious reader. You love immersing yourself in areas that interest you. Be that as it may, mere memorization and repetition bore you. You like challenging yourself intellectually. In fact, you will not hesitate to spend hour after hour sating your hunger for knowledge. For these reasons, you prefer applying your own thoughts and ideas to the new subjects you discover.

The 5 Greatest Areas of Improvement for an INTJ

Although you possess so many great qualities, there are also some things that you need to work on to achieve lasting happiness and success. Keep in mind that these are not limitations. These are opportunities for self-improvement.

1. Arrogance

When taken to the extreme, your high confidence can easily turn into arrogance. Although you are generally receptive to new ideas and suggestions, there might be times when you believe you have already resolved everything that needs to be resolved. When this happens, you might shut out the opinions of other people, especially those you feel intellectually superior to. If you find yourself doing this sometimes, it's important to remember that the opinions of other people are important too, even if they differ from your own.

2. Insensitive

INTJs are rational thinkers who value logic and reason. Emotions do not play a role in how you make decisions. This is why other people can sometimes see you as insensitive. Furthermore, you do not like sugarcoating things, making you blunt and direct. This can come across harshly to those with more sensitive personality types.

3. Uncomfortable in Rigid Environments

Although you possess an inclination toward judging, you frown upon blind followers. You have little respect for those who adhere to rules just for the sake of adherence. Being bound by guidelines that you do not personally agree with or understand is something that makes you feel extremely uncomfortable. This discomfort applies to all aspects of your life, be it company policies or social norms.

4. Dating Struggles

The unusual combination of your personality can sometimes make it difficult for you to dive into the world of dating. Your aversion to rules and social convention adds to this as well. Furthermore, your strategic thinking may lead you to constantly over-analyze every word and action of the person you're dating, which may strain your relationship.

5. Judgmental

You are a rational thinker, and you believe that something that is logical can't be wrong. Sometimes, this can cause you to be dismissive toward those you deem to be too emotional or illogical. There are even times when you might listen to other people's opinions and ideas with the sole agenda of finding fault.

What Makes an INTJ Happy?

As an INTJ, you are a strategic and intelligent individual who values logic and reason. You are able to view a situation from every possible vantage point, eliminating areas of inefficiency and embracing information that is useful. You are a natural strategist, and efficiency makes you extremely happy. When you find something that does not work as well as it should, you go out of your way to make it more efficient. That said, you hate it when resources are wasted and efforts are not maximized.

Whenever you encounter an idea that interests you, you will find ways to understand it as well as you can. You find great personal satisfaction in having your curiosity sated. You do this through research, analysis of data, and hours of reading. For an INTJ, the learning process never stops. You're always looking for new concepts to grasp, new information to study, and new approaches to try. In young INTJs, this quality is manifested through their love for reading. Being called a bookworm is a compliment for a young INTJ, because they truly enjoy expanding their knowledge about any subject. For these reasons, freedom is another thing that makes you happy. You want to be given the freedom to explore new opportunities and discover new things. Rigid rules and guidelines tend to get in the way of this, which is why you feel uncomfortable in environments that enforce such strict regulations.

Usually, INTJs have very high standards, especially when it comes to accomplishments and understanding of certain concepts. For this reason, you also have high standards for other people. You have great respect and appreciation for people whose knowledge and accomplishments surpass your own. You are happy to be able to learn from them and improve yourself in the process.

INTJs have little patience for social convention. You do not feel the need to be extremely polite all the time just because that is what's expected. You dislike small talk and shallow conversations. This does not mean you dislike all forms of social interaction. You just prefer genuine and meaningful interactions over those that barely break the surface. You do not see the value in being friendly just for the sake of being liked. As an introvert, you are happiest during moments of reflection that allow you to think and be introspective. As a result, you enjoy travelling alone and immersing yourself in new surroundings where you are free to explore and discover. You also enjoy solitary activities that utilize your strategic thinking, such as word games, puzzles, and Sudoku.

When it comes to relationships, you are happiest when you feel as though your ideas are appreciated and valued. You like surrounding yourself with people who understand your need for quiet, without shutting you out completely. In fact, you appreciate those who make the choice to just sit quietly with you. Because your personality type is so rare, you value people who accept you for who you are without wanting to change you. Furthermore, when you turn to a friend for advice during stressful situations, you do not want to be coddled. You're not just looking for a person to cry with. Rather, you want them to help you through meaningful advice. You want them to help you come to a decision in an objective and rational manner.

What are Some Common Careers of an INTJ?

One of your most remarkable qualities as an INTJ is your strategic mind. You possess the ability to look at a situation from every possible perspective. From there, you filter out the unnecessary information and focus on the areas that matter most. Whenever you look at something, you automatically try to see if there's a way to improve its efficiency. Furthermore, you are capable of understanding complex ideas and difficult concepts with ease. Because of this, you are likely to thrive in fields that utilize your intelligence and analytical skills, such as science and mathematics.

You are gifted in finding ways to streamline processes and speed up the way things are done. For you, efficiency is key. Jobs that allow you to do this as your primary focus will definitely appeal to you. A few examples are computer programming, software development, and computer science.

As a strategist, you see the effect one action will have on the outcome, and because of this, you are excellent at seeing the big picture and planning accordingly. Your strong intuition also guides you in coming up with strategies that will be helpful, even in the long haul. This quality will serve you extremely well in the fields of architecture and engineering. You are also likely to excel in the field of finance, as an accountant, financial manager, or budget consultant.

You also possess an insatiable hunger for knowledge. You love learning and discovering new things. A career in science will give you an avenue to utilize your curious nature and analytical mind. Chances are, you'll enjoy working as a scientist, chemist, or even as a historian. These jobs also appeal to your introverted nature, because these are jobs that are best done alone.

Your introverted nature is something that has to be considered when selecting a job. As an introvert, you prefer working alone. Your lone wolf approach to working is also a result of your high confidence in your own skills and abilities. For these reasons, it's unlikely that you will find satisfaction in careers that require working on a team with a large number of people. Some examples of careers that will give you the solitude you need are engineering, law, and as mentioned earlier, science.

Furthermore, social convention is not your strong suit. You dislike having to behave a certain way just because society says so. Because of this, it's probably a good idea to steer clear of jobs that require constant social interaction, such as jobs in customer service, public relations, and sales.

Overall, you will thrive in a workplace where you have the freedom to discover new things and utilize your skills in strategic thinking and problem solving. You work best on your own or with a small group of like-minded individuals.

Common Workplace Behaviors of an INTJ

INTJs are well known for being analytical, strategic, and rational. These qualities are very evident in everything you do, more so in the workplace. It does not matter which career path you choose, these characteristics will always shine through in the way you finish projects, handle stress, and solve problems.

In the workplace, you enjoy tasks that allow you to expand your existing body of knowledge regarding a certain subject. Broadening your expertise is something that you gain immense satisfaction from. You prefer positions that involve planning and making revisions to existing processes to make them more efficient. You naturally see opportunities for improvement within a system, and you are capable of coming up with different approaches to make things run more smoothly.

You enjoy things that are abstract and theoretical; however, you are most satisfied when your suggestions and implementations are utilized in a noticeable way. Your ideal work environment is one that is efficient, rational, and structured. You work best on your own, completing projects that require long periods of solitary analysis and concentration. You value your independence, and you take pride in your individual accomplishments and abilities. You want to be able to focus on the task at hand with as little interference as possible. That said, you are also able to work alongside a team of like-minded people if so required.

INTJs as Colleagues

When working on a team, you are great at defining team goals. You can take a complex idea and turn it into a feasible and achievable plan of action. You are very open-minded, and you embrace suggestions and ideas from other members of the team, as long as their ideas are logical and backed up by research. You prefer that your colleagues be as competent and productive as you are, and if they fall short of your expectations, you may lose respect for them. In fact, you may have a hard time getting along with colleagues whom you perceive as incompetent and inefficient. Logic is very important to you, and that's what you use to persuade other people to get on board with your plans. That said, you may experience some conflict with colleagues who do not value rational thinking as much as you do. You may think that such people slow down the work process. Personal connections rank very low on your list of priorities, and that's something that not everyone will understand. You find things like team-building exercises, regular meetings, and sugarcoated feedback unnecessary and annoying. You see these activities as wasteful and time-consuming.

INTJs as Employees

As an employee, you value your freedom. You are extremely independent, and you dislike being bound by strict rules and limitations. That's not to say you're disorganized. It's the opposite, in fact. You have a strong set of personal standards that you adhere to. You just want to be able to discover and explore on your own without the organization breathing down your neck. Furthermore, you find it hard to respect authority that you think is incompetent. That said, you think highly of those who prove to be capable, logical, and efficient. You appreciate managers who provide clear and constructive feedback and assess your performance in an objective manner.

INTJs as Supervisors

INTJs in leadership positions are firm, logical, and flexible. Although you are a natural leader, you are perfectly content to let someone else take the reins, as long as projects are carried out effectively. You value efficiency above everything else. Never should your team's efforts and resources go to waste. You are very rational, and because of your intuition, you have a clear vision of the things that need to get done and how to go about doing them. Unlike other judging types though, you are very flexible. You are okay with changing plans if the situation calls for it. This is also the reason you make sure that there are always back-up plans in case Plan A does not go as expected.

INTJ: Parenting Style and Values

INTJs may lack the warmth and affection of other personality types, but that does not mean you value relationships less. You just are not as expressive. You approach relationships in the same logical and strategic manner that you deal with almost everything else. You value independence — both your own and the people you're in a relationship with, and you do your best to keep the relationship moving in a positive direction.

As an INTJ, you want your children to become intelligent, capable, and independent individuals. In fact, this is probably your main goal as a parent. You want your children to make their own choices and learn from their mistakes. For that reason, you give your children ample space to discover and explore things on their own.

INTJs are not the most affectionate parents. Because your own need for physical reassurance is extremely low, you might be unable to sense this need in your children. Even though you love your children and want what's best for them, you might not be as sensitive to their emotional needs. You might not be able to tell if they're having a bad day or if they need some advice. You might not see hugs as a necessity. Because of this, you may need to turn to the other parent to fulfill your children's emotional needs.

That said, you are excellent at providing their physical needs. You make sure that they are always warm, fed, and taken care of. You also encourage your children to be independent. You do not coddle or restrict them too much. You want them to explore things, and it makes you happy when you see them discovering and learning new concepts. In fact, sharing knowledge is one of the ways you build a connection with your children. You enjoy teaching them things and showing them different perspectives. It's alright if they show interest in things that are unfamiliar to you, and you

49

show your love by being supportive of all their chosen endeavors.

It is likely that you have developed your own method or approach to parenting. You're not the kind of parent who will raise their kids a certain way just because that's how all the other parents are doing it. You are very confident with your parenting skills, and it's unlikely that you'll change your approach unless you see a really good reason to. Statements like "but everyone else's parents are letting them" do not sway you.

Because of your parenting style, your children will grow up to become independent and confident. They know that you will always be there to provide them with what they need, and this allows them to grow up feeling secure and safe. Even though they might not be showered with affection in the traditional sense of the word, they grow up knowing that they will be fed and taken care of, and that you will be there for them whatever happens. They will learn from your example and become self-sufficient and hardworking.

Why Do INTJs Make Good Friends?

INTJs tend to have more success in building and maintaining friendships than romantic relationships. That said, you may still encounter your fair share of challenges when it comes to connecting with other people. As an INTJ, you can be quite difficult to get to know. Furthermore, you're not the kind of person who will make an effort to get to know someone, especially if you feel as though they are on a different level. This is the reason why it's more likely to get along with someone who shares your intuitive (N) characteristic.

You have a very strong sense of what works and what does not. You know exactly what you like and what you do not like. While this might come across as arrogant or cocky, this is just how you filter the information around you so that you can focus on things that matter most. More than anything, you are looking for someone who can provide you with the intellectual stimulus that you require. You want deep conversations that have real meaning. Small talk and gossip do not interest you at all.

For these reasons, you are more likely to have only a handful of close friends, and that's exactly how you prefer it. You would rather build meaningful friendships with just a few people, than have many acquaintances that you do not really get along with. You do not like wasting time on people whom you feel do not have anything to offer you, intellectually that is.

When you become friends with someone, you do not require constant meetings or conversations to maintain that friendship. In fact, you encourage independence among your friends. You want them to live their lives while you live yours. Distance and lack of communication do not affect your closeness, as long as you have an intellectual connection. That said, you're probably the last person they should turn to for emotional support. Not because you do not care about them, but because you're so guarded about your own emotions that you might not know how to handle the feelings of other people. You prefer approaching problems rationally and logically.

As the friendship grows, you slowly learn how to relax and begin opening up. Especially if your friends are extroverts who are able to pull you out of your shell, you find yourself enjoying long conversations that are stimulating and meaningful. These are the times when your wit and humor shine through. Not everyone will understand your brand of humor though. This is why you are drawn to other intuitive types. They have the ability to read between the lines and understand you more.

INTJ Romance

INTJs are not known for their sensitivity and affection. In fact, most INTJs struggle with making connections with other people. You approach relationships with the same logic and rationality that you do most things in your life. When it comes to romance, you have a predetermined action plan which you hope will achieve the end goal: a stable and healthy relationship.

Unlike most personality types, the term "falling in love" does not seem to apply to you. You assess potential partners using a personal set of criteria. If they pass, you can then proceed to the next step of the relationship, then the next, then the next. In a perfect, logic-driven world, this might work. However, relationships rarely fit an exact mold. This makes finding a significant other quite difficult for INTJs.

It can be said that feelings are an INTJ's Achilles heel. Things that are considered romantic and sweet by other people might be seen as unnecessary and silly by an INTJ. You're not naturally attuned to your own emotions, let alone the emotions of other people. As a result, you can sometimes seem insensitive and cold. This causes you to hurt your partner's feelings even if you do not mean to. It's important to remember the impact your words and actions can have on the people you care about. Keep in mind that your partner has emotional needs and that your relationship is more than just a puzzle to be analyzed.

When it comes to intimacy, you may have the tendency to spend more time thinking about it than actually doing it. However, INTJs who are aware of the importance of such displays are more likely to be comfortable with showing affection. Over time, you will learn the value of romantic gestures and verbal affirmations, and will incorporate these in your approach to relationships. That said, other INTJ's might end up thinking that the effort isn't worth it.

They might conclude that there's no one out there that can match them intellectually, which will make finding a mate even more difficult.

The strange thing about INTJs is that you tend to draw the attention of more people when you are not trying so hard. This is because your intelligence and confidence shine through in a positive manner when you're more relaxed. As a result, your best bet for finding someone to share your life with is by letting them approach you instead of seeking them out.

When you find someone you have made a connection with, you will do everything you can to work toward a healthy and stable relationship. Because you value efficiency and are always looking for ways to improve things, you never stop trying to make your relationship even stronger. As a partner, you are enthusiastic and stimulating, especially if your significant other shares your passion for discovering and exploring new things.

You strive to create a deep and meaningful bond with your partner, both physically and intellectually.

Even when you find yourself in a happy and stable relationship, you never stop valuing your independence. You still want room to grow on your own. You also want your partner to be independent as well. You want them to live their own lives while you live yours. Of course, you enjoy being able to share things with them, but you also want them to respect your need for privacy and solitude.

During moments of conflict, you tend to see things as a puzzle or mind game that needs to be solved. There are even times when you might enjoy the process of looking for a solution to the problems in your relationship. This can be a good thing, because as a strategist, you look for answers that are mutually beneficial for all parties involved. However, you also need to understand that some feelings should be expressed just for the sake of expressing them. Keep in mind that venting or letting out emotions can be very therapeutic for other personality types.

Best Relationship Matches for an INTJ

While it's true that two people can build a lasting relationship regardless of personality type, there are some types that are more compatible with others. For INTJs, the most compatible matches are ENTPs and ENFPs.

The extroverted personality of an ENTP or ENFP will be able to pull you out of your shell and allow you to open up more. Their outgoing demeanor will also make it easier for you to be more comfortable around them. Furthermore, it's necessary that you find someone who shares your intuitive trait. Because you can be quite difficult to read, their ability to read between the lines will make communication easier. Sharing the (N) trait also increases the chances of creating an almost instantaneous connection, which is something you will not be likely to find with sensing types. Their perceiving trait will keep your relationship exciting and stimulating, which appeals to your passion for exploration and discovery. ENTPs are a good match because you both share the thinking trait, but ENFPs can teach you how to be more in touch with your emotions. That said, both of those personality types are good matches for you.

Weaknesses

- Seeing Things as a Puzzle - You tend to see your relationship as something like a puzzle that has to be solved. During moments of conflict, you are more focused looking for a rational solution than pacifying your partner's feelings. For this reason, your partner may feel misunderstood or not cared for.
- Lack of Affection - While you compensate for your lack of affection through other ways, some partners

may not be able to translate your actions as displays of love and concern. Especially for those that need constant affirmation, your reserved nature might be misperceived as a lack of interest.

- Insensitive - You do not possess the natural intuition of other personality types. You are not able to sense what your partner is feeling. This can make you seem insensitive at times. This can be overcome by paying attention to your partner's gestures and words to look for signs about what they're feeling.

Strengths

- Honesty - You do not possess the natural intuition of other personality types. You are not able to sense what your partner is feeling. This can make you seem insensitive at times. This can be overcome by paying attention to your partner's gestures and words to look for signs about what they're feeling.

- Good Practical Skills - Because of the judging preference of your personality, you are excellent at handling the practical things in a relationship. Things such as planning and budgeting are your forte. You know how to plan the perfect vacation while staying within budget. You also make sure that your day-to-day lives run smoothly.

- Ability to Remain Rational - You do not possess the natural intuition of other personality types. You are not able to sense what your partner is feeling. This can make you seem insensitive at times. This can be overcome by paying attention to your partner's gestures and words to look for signs about what they're feeling.

7 Actionable Steps for Overcoming Your Weaknesses as an INTJ

Now that you have identified and recognized the things that you can improve about your personality, where do you begin? The following steps can help you overcome your weaknesses and become a better and happier person.

1. Be More Sensitive

You see social convention as unnecessary and a waste of time. However, some people are more sensitive than others, and there's nothing you can do but be more aware of how your actions and words can have an impact on others. Your honesty can be quite extreme to the more emotional types, and you might end up hurting their feelings even if you do not mean to. Before you share your direct and unfiltered opinions, try to ask yourself if it's something that might be interpreted as hurtful or offensive and adjust your delivery accordingly. This does not mean you have to stop being honest. Just try to phrase things in a more positive and encouraging manner.

2. Remember That People's Opinions Are Valid Too

In general, you have no problems with accepting other people's opinions and ideas, as long as they are backed up by research and logic. However, you have the tendency to ignore the opinions of people who are not as smart as you are. Keep in mind that everyone has something to bring to the table. Even though you may be more competent than they are in a certain field, they may have a fresh perspective that you might have overlooked. Furthermore, respecting other people's opinions is essential in building meaningful connections.

3. Place Yourself in Other People's Shoes

You hold yourself to extremely high standards. This goes for other people too. You expect them to behave as logically and rationally as you do. You believe that they should complete tasks with the same efficiency that you do. However, it's important to remember that not everyone sees things the same way that you do. Next time you find yourself getting impatient because someone has failed to live up to your expectations, place yourself in their shoes and try seeing things from their vantage point.

4. Be Humble

Although your self-confidence is a remarkable quality, this can sometimes turn into arrogance. Keep in mind that you are human, and therefore, fallible. Even though you may be an expert at what you do, there's always room for improvement. There are always new things to discover. There are always new ways to improve yourself. Learn how to be humble. Know that you are not immune to making mistakes, and that's okay.

5. Learn How to Delegate

You prefer working alone, because you have the tendency to believe that you're the only person who knows how to get the job done. This can sometimes cause you to take on too much at once. Learn how to delegate. Pay more attention to other people's strengths and abilities, and let them handle things from time to time. You would be more efficient that way. Know that not everything is your sole responsibility.

6. Learn How to Loosen Up

You have your own way of doing certain things, and it's hard for you to deviate from your plans and schedules unless there's a compelling reason to. Loosen up a little. You can start with something small. Take a different route to work tomorrow morning. Eat lunch at a different restaurant this afternoon. Try an activity you have never tried before. You would be surprised by how fun and enjoyable new experiences can be, even if there's no logical reason for doing them.

7. Do Not Over-Analyze

Your strategic mind is always at work. You are constantly looking for problems to solve and puzzles to complete. While this quality is extremely useful in some parts of your life, it does not work as well when it comes to friendships and relationships. Treating personal connections as puzzles may cause other people to feel as though you do not care about their feelings. When a friend or loved one comes to you during stressful moments, take a step back and just let them vent. Let them air out their feelings without offering to help them fix the situation. Most of the time, they just want to know that you're there for them.

The 10 Most Influential INTJs We Can Learn From

INTJs are gifted individuals whose intelligence and problem-solving skills are unparalleled. Here are a few examples of INTJs who have inspired and influenced people all over the world.

1. Isaac Newton

Isaac Newton was an English mathematician and scientist. He is considered one of the most influential people of all time and was responsible for many important scientific discoveries. In fact, influential is an understatement. Aside from the laws of motion that he is best known for, Newton also contributed to the fields of optics, mathematics, and astronomy.

2. Ayn Rand

Ayn Rand was a novelist who is best known for her novel, *Atlas Shrugged*. Like a true INTJ, Rand was an advocate for logic and reason, and she rejected religion and faith because of the lack of rationality. Another INTJ trait that Rand was known for is her unwavering confidence in her beliefs and accomplishments.

3. Friedrich Nietzsche

Friedrich Nietzsche was a German philosopher, poet, and cultural critic. He is best known for his objective approach and rational thinking. In fact, his theories have steadily been influencing scholars and laymen all over the world.

4. Mark Zuckerberg

Mark Zuckerberg is best known as the CEO of Facebook, the largest social media website of today. He is a computer programmer, which is an ideal career for INTJs. Mark Zuckerberg is an excellent example of an INTJ who used his skills in strategic planning to make a name for himself.

5. Bobby Fischer

Bobby Fischer was a chess prodigy who quit school at the age of sixteen. According to him, the reason he quit school was that he felt like he was surrounded by people of lesser intelligence. He went on to become the greatest chess player of all time.

6. Stephen Hawking

Stephen Hawking is a cosmologist and theoretical physicist. In an interview, he once said that his only goal was a complete grasp of the universe. He is another example of an INTJ who used his analytical skills to change the world we live in. He is the author of the book *A Brief History of Time*.

7. Nikola Tesla

Nikola Tesla was an inventor and engineer who is best known for his contributions to electrical engineering. His inventions have changed the world in so many tangible ways.

8. Isaac Asimov

Isaac Asimov was a biochemistry professor and author who is best known for his science fiction novels and stories. He possessed a remarkable understanding of science and mathematics, which allowed him to write his books in an inimitable way.

9. Jean-Paul Sartre

Jean-Paul Sartre was a philosopher, novelist, and political activist who is best known for his intellectual participation in a number of fields. He also authored the book *Being and Nothingness* which talks about human nature and freedom.

10. James Cameron

James Cameron is a film director and producer who is best known for his films such as *The Terminator* and *Aliens*. He is seen by others as a perfectionist, and some people describe his approach to directing as mechanical and quite dictatorial.

Conclusion

As an INTJ, you are a systematic and analytical individual who possesses an intelligent and strategic mind. You value your privacy and you work best on your own. You possess the ability to see the larger picture, and you can see a situation from every perspective possible. You make decisions based on logic and reason, and you operate most efficiently in an ordered and structured environment.

You have a number of remarkable qualities. You are intelligent and quick-witted. You are honest and straightforward. You are also a gifted analyst and problem solver. Identifying these strengths will help you on your journey toward success and happiness. That said, there are also some qualities that can be improved. Your honesty can sometimes come across as insensitive. Your confidence can be misconstrued as arrogance. You also have the tendency to dismiss people who are too emotional or sensitive. Keep in mind that you have the ability to overcome these weaknesses and become a better, well-rounded individual.

When selecting a career, choose jobs that will highlight your natural strengths. Careers in the fields of engineering, science, and mathematics are excellent choices, because they enable you to utilize your intelligence and analytical skills. It's also helpful to steer clear of jobs that require extended periods of social interaction, such as customer service and sales. The amount of dialogue required in those jobs might be too exhausting for an introvert like you. Furthermore, you find social convention exhausting and unnecessary.

Be a little more sensitive. Try not to be too critical of other people's shortcomings. Remember, we are all human and prone to making mistakes. Put yourself in other people's shoes to see things from their point of view. As proven by many other INTJs, you are capable of great things, if you put your mind to it.

Everything you have read so far is meant to give you a look into the inner workings of your mind. That said, this is by no means a comprehensive guide that dictates what you should or should not do. This is merely a guide that will help you find your place in the world and eventually achieve success and happiness.

Final Word/About the Author

I was born and raised in Norwalk, Connecticut. Growing up, I could often be found spending afternoons reading in the local public library about management techniques and leadership styles, along with overall outlooks towards life. It was from spending those afternoons reading about how others have led productive lives that I was inspired to start studying patterns of human behavior and self-improvement. Usually I write works around sports to learn more about influential athletes in the hopes that from my writing, you the reader can walk away inspired to put in an equal if not greater amount of hard work and perseverance to pursue your goals. However, I began writing about psychology topics such as the Myers Brigg Type Indicator so that I could help others better understand why they act and think the way they do and how to build on their strengths while also identifying their weaknesses. If you enjoyed

INTJ: Understanding & Relating with the Mastermind please leave a review! Also, you can read more of my works on ISTJs, ISFJs, ISFPs, INFPs, ESFPs, ESFJs, ESTJs, ENFPs, ENFJs, *How to be Witty, How to be Likeable, How to be Creative, Bargain Shopping, Productivity Hacks, Morning Meditation, Becoming a Father,* and *33 Life Lessons: Success Principles, Career Advice & Habits of Successful People* in the Kindle Store.

Like what you read?

If you love books on life, basketball, or productivity, check out my website at claytongeoffreys.com to join my exclusive list where I let you know about my latest books. Aside from being the first to hear about my latest releases, you can also download a free copy of *33 Life Lessons: Success Principles, Career Advice & Habits of Successful People.* See you there!

Printed in Great
Britain
by Amazon